THE TALE OF
MR TOD

A story about two disagreeable people
called Tommy Brock and Mr Tod

From the authorized animated series
based on the original tales
BY **BEATRIX POTTER**™
F. WARNE & CO

Old Mr Bouncer sat in the spring sunshine outside the burrow, in a muffler, smoking a pipe of rabbit tobacco.

Old Mr Bouncer was stricken in years. He lived with his son Benjamin Bunny and his daughter-in-law Flopsy, who had a young family.

"Now take care of the children Uncle Bouncer," said Flopsy, "we're going out visiting for a while."

The little rabbit-babies were just old enough to open their blue eyes and kick. They lay in a fluffy bed of rabbit wool and hay, in a shallow burrow, separate from the main rabbit hole. To tell the truth – old Mr Bouncer had forgotten them.

Tommy Brock was passing through the woods, with a sack and a little spade which he used for digging, and some mole traps. He was looking for food. Tommy Brock was friendly with old Mr Bouncer; they agreed in disliking Mr Tod.

Old Mr Bouncer sat in the sun, and conversed cordially with Tommy Brock. "What's the news from down hill, Tommy my dear fellow?" said Mr Bouncer. "Not so good I'm sorry to say," said Tommy Brock, "I have not had a good square meal in a fortnight. I shall have to turn vegetarian and eat my own tail!" It was not much of a joke, but old Mr Bouncer laughed.

"My dear old chap, won't you step inside for a slice of seed cake and a glass of homemade cowslip wine to fortify the constitution," he said.

3

Tommy Brock squeezed himself into the rabbit hole with alacrity. "Have a cabbage leaf cigar, Tommy, go on," said old Mr Bouncer, who was smoking his pipe. Smoke filled the burrow. Old Mr Bouncer coughed and laughed; and Tommy Brock puffed and grinned.

Mr Bouncer laughed and coughed. "I don't get many visitors, not like it used to be," he mumbled sleepily. He slumped lower in his chair and shut his eyes because of the cabbage smoke . . .

Tommy Brock waited a few moments to be sure that old Mr Bouncer was fast asleep. Then he put all the young rabbit-babies into his sack.

When Flopsy and Benjamin came back – old Mr Bouncer woke up. "Uncle Bouncer, where are the children?" said Flopsy, anxiously. "Father, where are the babies?" asked Benjamin. But Mr Bouncer would not confess that he had admitted anybody into the rabbit hole.

The smell of badger was undeniable, and there were round heavy footmarks in the sand. Mr Bouncer was in disgrace; Flopsy wrung her ears, and slapped him. "It's old Tommy Brock, he's taken our babies," she cried.

"Now don't worry, Flopsy," said Benjamin, "I'll catch that old rogue." Benjamin Bunny set off at once after Tommy Brock.

There was not much difficulty in tracking him; Benjamin soon found his footmarks. He had gone slowly up the winding footpath through the

wood, and his heavy steps showed plainly in the mud.

The path led to a part of the thicket where the trees
had been cleared; there were leafy oak stumps, and a
sea of blue hyacinths – but the smell that made
Benjamin stop, was *not* the smell of flowers!

Mr Tod's stick house was before him and, for once,

Mr Tod was
at home.
Inside the
stick house
somebody
dropped a
plate, and said
something.
Benjamin
stamped his
foot, and
bolted.
He never
stopped until he came to the
other side of the wood.

Apparently Tommy Brock
had turned the same way.
Upon the top of the wall,
some ravellings of a sack had
caught on a bramble bush.

It was getting late in the afternoon. Other rabbits were coming out to enjoy the evening air. "Cousin Peter! Peter Rabbit, Peter Rabbit!" shouted Benjamin Bunny. "Whatever is the matter, Cousin Benjamin?" asked Peter. "He's bagged my family – Tommy Brock – in a sack, have you seen him?"

Peter had seen Tommy Brock, carrying a sack with "something live in it".

"Cousin Benjamin, compose yourself," he said. "Tommy Brock has gone to Mr Tod's other house at the top of Bull Banks."

And Peter accompanied the afflicted parent, who was all of a twitter. "Hurry Peter; he will be cooking them; come quicker!" said Benjamin Bunny.

Tommy Brock was already in Mr Tod's kitchen, making preparations for supper. (Mr Tod had half a dozen houses, but he was seldom at home. The houses were not always empty when Mr Tod moved *out*; because sometimes Tommy Brock moved *in*, without asking leave).

The sunshine was still warm and slanting on the hill pastures. Half way up, Cotton-tail was sitting in her doorway, with four or five half-grown little rabbits playing about her; one black and the others brown. She had

seen Tommy Brock passing. He had rested nearby a while, pointed to the sack, and seemed doubled up with laughing.

"Squirrel Nutkin, have you seen Tommy Brock?" asked Peter. But he hadn't.

9

In the wood at Bull Banks, the trees grew amongst heaped up rocks; and there, beneath a crag – Mr Tod had made one of his homes.

The rabbits crept up carefully, listening and peeping. The setting sun made the window panels glow like red flame; but the kitchen fire was not alight. Benjamin sighed with relief. No person was to be seen, and no young rabbits. But the preparations for one person's supper on the table made him shudder.

Then they scrambled round to the other side of the house, and crept up

to the bedroom window. As their eyes became accustomed to the darkness, they perceived that somebody was asleep, lying under a blanket. Tommy Brock's snores came, grunty and regular, from Mr Tod's bed.

They went back to the front of the house, and tried in every way to move the bolt of the kitchen window. They tried to push up a rusty nail between the window sashes; but it was of no use, especially without a light.

In half an hour the moon rose over the wood, and shone full and clear and cold, in at the kitchen window. The light showed a little door beside the kitchen fireplace, belonging to a brick oven. Presently Peter and Benjamin noticed that whenever they shook the window, the little door opposite shook in answer. The young family were alive, shut up in the oven!

They sat side by side outside the window, whispering. There was really not very much comfort in the discovery. Although the young family was alive, the little rabbits were quite incapable of letting themselves out; they were not old enough to crawl.

After much debate, Peter and Benjamin decided to dig a tunnel. "It's the only way. A tunnel right under the house, and into the kitchen." They began to burrow a yard or two lower down the bank. They dug and dug for hours and hours. They could not tunnel straight on account of stones; but by the end of the night they were under the kitchen floor. It was morning – sunrise.

From the fields down below there came the angry cry of a jay – followed by the sharp yelping bark of a fox! Then those two rabbits lost their heads completely. They did the most foolish thing that they could have done. They rushed into their short new tunnel, and hid themselves at the top end of it, under Mr Tod's kitchen floor.

Mr Tod was coming up Bull Banks, and he was in the very worst of tempers. "Badger . . . Badger . . . I can smell Badger," he fumed, and slapped his stick upon the earth; he guessed where Tommy Brock had gone to.

Mr Tod approached his house very carefully with a large rusty key, and went in. The sight of the table all set out for supper made him furious. But what absorbed Mr Tod's attention was a noise – a deep slow regular snoring grunting noise, coming from his own bed. He peeped around the half-open bedroom door.

Mr Tod came out of the house in a hurry; he scratched up the earth with fury. His whiskers bristled and his coat-collar stood on end with rage. "Badger . . . Badger . . . in my house, in my bed, I'll fix that Badger." He fetched a clothes line and went back into the bedroom.

He stood a minute watching Tommy Brock and listening to the loud snores. Then Mr Tod turned his back towards the bed and undid the window. It creaked; he turned round with a jump. Tommy Brock, who had opened one eye – shut it hastily. The snores continued. Mr Tod pushed the greater part of the clothes line out of the window.

Mr Tod went out at the front door, and round to the back of the house. He took up the coil of line from the window sill, listened for a moment, (Tommy Brock snored conscientiously), and then tied the rope to a tree. "I will wake him with an unpleasant surprise," he said.

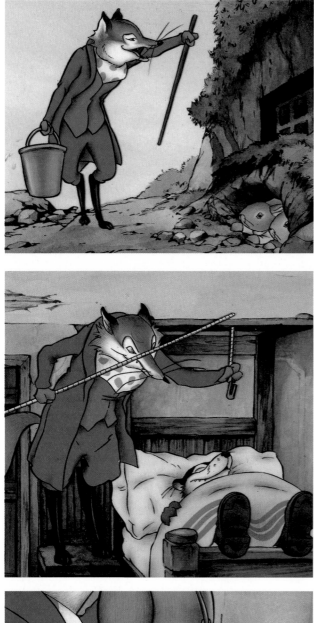

Mr Tod fetched a large heavy pailful of water from the spring, and staggered with it through the kitchen into his bedroom. Tommy Brock snored industriously, with rather a snort. He was lying on his back with his mouth open, grinning from ear to ear. One eye was still not perfectly shut.

Then Mr Tod put down the pail, and took up the end of the rope with a hook attached. He gingerly mounted a chair by the head of the bedstead. His legs were dangerously near to Tommy Brock's teeth. He reached up and put the end of rope over the head of the bed, where the curtains ought to hang.

Mr Tod, who was a thin-legged person (though vindictive and sandy whiskered) – was quite unable to lift the heavy weight of the full pail of water to the level of the hook and rope. After much thought he emptied the water into a wash-basin and jug.

The empty pail was not too heavy for him; he slung it up wobbling over the head of Tommy Brock. Surely there never was such a sleeper!
Mr Tod got up and down, down and up on the chair.

As he could not lift the whole pailful of water at once, he fetched a milk jug, and ladled quarts of water into the pail by degrees. The pail got fuller and fuller, and swung like a pendulum. Occasionally a drop splashed over; but still Tommy Brock snored regularly and never moved – except one eye.

At last Mr Tod's preparations were complete. "It will make a great mess in my bedroom; but I could never sleep in that bed again without a spring cleaning of some sort," said Mr Tod, and softly left the room. He ran round behind the house, to the tree. He was obliged to gnaw the rope with his teeth – he chewed and gnawed for more then twenty minutes.

The moment he had gone, Tommy Brock got up in a hurry. He peered out of the window and saw Mr Tod

gnawing on the rope.

Tommy Brock rolled Mr Tod's dressing-gown into a bundle, put it into the bed beneath the pail of water instead of himself, and left the room also – grinning immensely. He went into the kitchen, lighted the fire and boiled the kettle; for the moment he did not trouble himself to cook the baby rabbits.

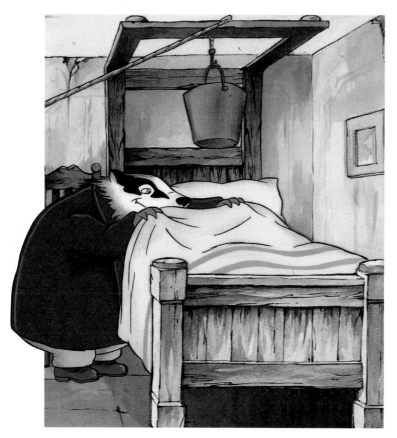

18

At last the rope snapped. Inside the house there was a great crash and splash.

But no screams. Mr Tod listened attentively. Then he peeped in at the window. In the middle of the bed under the blanket, was a wet flattened *something* – its head was covered by the wet blanket and it was *not snoring any longer*. Mr Tod's eyes glistened. "This has turned out even better than I expected," said Mr Tod. "I will bury that nasty person in a hole. I will have a thorough disinfecting with soap to remove the smell." He hurried round the house to get a shovel . . .

. . . He opened the door . . . Tommy Brock was sitting at Mr Tod's kitchen table, pouring tea from Mr Tod's tea-pot into Mr Tod's tea-cup. He was quite dry, and he was grinning. He threw a cup of scalding tea all over Mr Tod.

Then Mr Tod rushed upon Tommy Brock, and Tommy Brock grappled with Mr Tod amongst the broken crockery, and there was a terrific battle all over the kitchen. To the rabbits underneath, it sounded as if the floor would give way at each crash of falling furniture.

Inside the house the racket was fearful. The rabbit babies in the oven woke up trembling; perhaps it was fortunate they were shut up inside. Everything was broken; the crockery was smashed to atoms. Tommy Brock put his foot in a jar of raspberry jam.

The kettle fell off the hob, and the boiling water out of the kettle fell upon the tail of Mr Tod. Tommy Brock rolled Mr Tod over and over like a log, out at the door.

"Let's get out of here, Benjamin," said Peter. The two rabbits crept out of their tunnel, and hung about amongst the rocks and bushes, listening anxiously.

Tommy Brock and Mr Tod rolled over and over. The snarling and worrying went on, and they rolled over the bank, and down hill, bumping over the rocks. There would never be any love lost between Tommy Brock and Mr Tod.

As soon as the coast was clear, Peter Rabbit and Benjamin Bunny came out of the bushes – "Run for it! Run in, Cousin Benjamin! Run in and get them! While I watch the door."

In Mr Tod's kitchen, amongst the wreckage, Benjamin Bunny picked his way to the oven nervously, through a thick cloud of dust. He opened the oven door, felt inside, and found something warm and

wriggling. He lifted it out carefully, and rejoined Peter Rabbit outside.

At home in the rabbit hole, things had not been quite comfortable.

After quarrelling at supper, Flopsy and old Mr Bouncer had passed a sleepless night, and quarrelled again at breakfast.

Old Mr Bouncer could no longer deny that he had invited company into the rabbit

hole, but he refused to reply to the questions and reproaches of Flopsy. The day passed heavily.

The two breathless rabbits came scuttering away down Bull Banks, Benjamin half carrying, half dragging a sack, bumpetty bump over the grass. They reached home safely and burst into the rabbit hole.

Great was old Mr Bouncer's relief and Flopsy's joy when Peter and Benjamin arrived in triumph with the young family. "Benjamin, Peter – oh, thank goodness you're all safe," said Flopsy.
"I was a bit worried myself, actually," admitted Mr Bouncer.

Old Mr Bouncer was forgiven. The rabbit-babies were rather tumbled and very hungry; they were fed and put to bed. They soon recovered. Then Peter and Benjamin told their story – but they had not waited long enough to be able to tell the end of the battle between Tommy Brock and Mr Tod.

THE END